A TRIBUTE TO NIPSEY HUSSLE (ERMIAS ASGHEDOM)

~Nipsey Hussle Lockdown Society Dedication~

By Hitachi Choparazzi

A TRIBUTE TO NIPSEY HUSSLE (ERMIAS ASGHEDOM)
~Nipsey Hussle Lockdown Society Dedication~
©Copyright 2020
All Rights Reserved
By Hitachi Choparazzi
Chop-A-Style Publishing LLC
Cover by: Skylar "Scky Rei" Reed @sckyrei
LCCN:2022902460
ISBN: 979-8-9857661-6-5

Acknowledgements

I'd like to acknowledge Ermias Asghedom, AKA Nipsey Hussle the Great, spirit and everlasting vibrant energy and influence. Nipsey's friends, family, and N-Hood. His Mom, Dad, Grandma, Sis, Blacc Sam, Emani, Kross, and Lauren London. All his works, arts, music, and community support and ties. #TMC

My sons and daughter. My fans, family, GMA Lawson and all my loved ones and day ones that passed on—Rest in Harmony. Chop-a-Style Publishing. IncarceratedLivesMatter.com #ILM. BillionDollarBluePrintMovement.com #BDB. And of course all of lockdown society and our push/movement. #FreeHitachiChoparazzi Hitachichoparazziauthor@gmail.com

Prologue

March 31st. 2019...Nipsey Hussle the Great tweets under *Victory Lap*–VLICON:

"Having strong enemies is a blessing."

That last day of March in Compton, California, breezy spring air on Crenshaw and Slauson Ave. sat the Marathon Clothing store in the middle of Nipsey's shopping plaza. The Cali recreational kush could be smelled loud as it plagued the parking lot.

Nipsey pushed outside the Marathon store fearless with 2 luv1s mid-day. One who was fresh out after 20 years. Nipsey had to show his luv as always reintegrating his luv1s and community.

Then Nip's name was called out from a short distance behind him.

Sporadic shots rang out, echoing throughout the plaza as people scrambled and screamed frantically.

Nipsey Hussle dropped along with his loved ones on the pavement as pandemonium ensued.

"Ya got me, cuhz...I'm gud," was Nipsey Hussle's last words before more shots rang out. Nipsey was shot a total of 6 times before a car door slammed and screeched out the parking lot erratically.

The ambulance rushed Nipsey Hussle to the hospital where shortly after a fight for his life, he was pronounced dead.

The breaking news on social media, T.V., radio, and lockdown society of Nip's untimely sudden demise spread fast like wildfire. The nation sat in silence, outraged and mourning.

The music lives on vibrant globally.

"Last time I checked it was 5 chains on my neck—it was no smut on my rep!" Nipsey Hussle—*Victory Lap*

The whole world was shocked and showed love. Buying Crenshaw merch, celebrities and fans streaming Nip's songs internationally. Even people that never heard Nip's music or knew who he was and his movement was still moved.

Then you began to hear the love and Nipsey Hussle's music everywhere. In arenas, T.V., stadiums, radio, venues, etc.

"I ain't need radio to do mine, I did fine." Nipsey Hussle—*Last Time I Checked*

Lockdown society was crushed but lit with all the love Nipsey was receiving and all the play he was getting throughout the world. Because he can relate and came from same background. Also rep the struggle with us incarcerated. I wanted to be the voice of locked-down society, pay homage and respect to Nipsey with the rest of the luv1s on the inside and do a tribute to Nipsey. Reflect his life, music, works and significant impact on the inside, too. This is our dedication.

#TheMarathonContinues

R.I.P. N-Hood NIP!

Contents

- Chapter 1 -

"Dedication"

Life is not a sprint...it's a marathon.

This book is a dedication tribute to the late Ermias "Nipsey Hussle" Asghedom the Great, 8-15-85 to 3-31-19. Rest in Harmony. May your torch and legacy stay lit. The baton passed on for generations to the relay and the marathon continues with everlasting perpetual progress and empowerment.

"Dedication, hard work, plus patience—dedication." Nipsey Hussle—*Dedication*

All money in, no money out...had the whole Penn buzzing. Nipsey Hussle was vibrant. His energy throughout lockdown society just from his music and videos alone. Everyone that listened to Nipsey's music on the inside knew what he was spitting was facts. And even if you didn't know his music, you still knew he spit truth and the culture most of us lived or came directly from. Also still part of it trying to break through and transform.

I had to step up and speak out. Be the voice of appreciation inside and show our gratitude and pay homage. Let the world know about Nipsey Hussle prison reform influence, impact, assistance on showing us a positive outlet and blueprint to follow. Also to reflect Nipsey's greatness and how unified rivals became inside working together building blueprints, movements, and music.

Without outside support, a voice, platform, an outlet, most people don't have nothing to lose or look forward to hopeless, which usually develops into a fuck-it type attitude. They are numb to a lot once that outside connection is lost. Even after a relative passes away. It's no true imminent feelings there.

Through some hardships to overcome, people go to religion and faith, searching for higher elevation or to be grounded. Circumstances shape but don't define us. Even though society outcasts incarcerated lives. Some people use God to transform them into their peak greatness. Others music, workouts, reading, and writing as therapy to transcend within. Self-reform with meditation and prayers.

"Shout out to my niggas in the Penn text messaging." Nipsey Hussle—*Key to the City*

Nipsey said he should have been on a level 4 yard with his homies. We all knew it was vibrant facts, and Nip cared about his luvıs in locked-down society.

Lockdown society and our culture needs to see somebody that looks like them. That can relate to their struggle to overcome, defy all odds, and arise above to a success story.

Nipsey was our hero and relatable most to us. He had a way of influence and bringing people into his greatness, showing you can be great, too. It's highly possible with hard work and dedication.

He also made it cool to be hoodsmart (hood/booksmart). How to shift, rebuild your mind, and rebrand yourself. Own all your rights, properties, and all that you self-build. Surrounding yourself by others in that way you want to be in your likeness to flourish for betterment.

"Weight on my shoulders bring best out—nigga...I don't stress out, nigga, I poke my chest out—nigga." Nipsey Hussle

Nip said his big bro Blacc Sam told him to poke his chest out. And Nipsey loved adversity and embraced it as a challenge.

Setbacks and adversity help you thrive, if you use it. Not as isolation. Some things can take years to get thru and on track. Nipsey knew this and stayed focused and consistent. He also inspired lockdown society to get better and be a better them. To find themselves, believe self, and dream to accomplish their life task and act on it. Discovery and decision is key to your revolution of gift or greatness in your potential.

Which Nipsey Hussle the Great left the youth, people, and future generations space to create.

"Ship you out of town, now you need a pen pal." Nipsey Hussle

A lot of us suffer from not just disconnection from society and loved ones. But depression, trying to fill a void, no passion, purpose, and miserable. We want passion, driven cause, feel love and support, and a sense of belonging. Especially on that righteous path of reforming.

When being incarcerated, finding your true self, learning to rebuild, adjustment, and growth is your innate process. Usually with appreciation and acknowledgement through social betterment and support helps you to reinvent yourself and taking on aspiration for a new look and identity.

Nipsey Hussle fought for equality, justice, and used a platform for it.

It's always been out of sight, out of mind with prison reform... now a spotlight is being shined heavily on it with more people, organizations, celebrities using their platforms.

Visuals make things matter and everything in our today society. We highly thankful for Nipsey never forgetting about us incarcerated and using his platform to shine light back on us. And having an idea or vision for ourselves, bringing it to life by grinding it out being passionate, focused on your opportunity with dedication and hard work. Regardless of the labor-intense, time-consuming, merciless devoted self-discipline.

Then showed us if we don't know much, we can't do much. So we knowing we don't have control of much. However, we started using time *for* us, versus *against* us. Which we started making our time work for us. Discovering our genius and developing content and creating value out of our content. Self-reforming, self-building, and self-rehabilitation are all our process of self-awareness and self-consciousness as tools, power tools cognitive.

Nipsey Hussle had the ability to inspire us and the youth to show us we important and relevant and have the ability to push and opportunity to create our own space, finding your niche column. It's not how smart you are...it's how are you smart?

Now we discovering techniques and strategies to use effectively to master our super-powers to push the energy, furthering the marathon of betterment.

Leaders are readers. Nipsey would read books, give people books to read, and recommend certain books for us to build and read. Usually empowerment, self-help or a how-to book. They say the average person reads 2 to 4 books a year. And the average CEO reads 4 to 6 books a month. Now the whole lockdown society has a read list, not just a playlist anymore. All thanks to Nipsey Hussle.

His time and energy will forever be sustainability for us forever on this Earth, especially as a format and blueprint. The face of it. So we are forever dedicated to the marathon and Nipsey Hussle cause and movement. This book is a whole dedication, love, and respect for Ermias "Nipsey Hussle" Asghedom the Great, not just this chapter. A creator and innovator. An influencer and motivator. A visionary and humanitarian. A revolutionary and activist. A mogul and a philanthropist. The Tupac of the West and his timeline. Most of all infamous legendary moves, all money in, no money out, and teaching how to charge more than what they told you. Showing people their self-worth and how to demand your worth of your works itself.

Which Nipsey valuing his self-worth of his CD for $100 each led to Jay Z and Roc Nation recognizing him and respecting his hustle, buying 100 CDs, supporting Nipsey's valuation and perspective. Which shocked the world but not Nipsey. It didn't deter him with all the hate and naysayers. No, it just fueled him to keep on his marathon. And later on he met Jay Z and they collaborated together, teaming up. He even did a Jay Z sample on his latest *Victory Lap* album.

Nipsey Hussle wasn't a clout chaser. He was the clout that everyone was chasing and rappers fictitiously rapped about. He stood out and never tried to fit in. You couldn't imitate his swift and smooth immaculate moves. Especially how he loved to move in silence and producing, letting his actions speak volumes for him. And to this very day people still discovering and learning more things about Nipsey and what he was a part of and had his hands all in on. From donating to schools and creating a school program to help inner-city minority youth learn more about science and computer science. He would employ the community and help the homeless, feeding them without judging them or turning a blind eye. He had so many stories of how he helped homeless people clean up and giving them a job from cutting hair to working in his neighborhood around him.

"If you don't die here—you suppose to fly Leer." Nipsey Hussle

We still hear Nipsey Hussle's infectious words and music. They still have an influential vibrant everlasting effect. More than ever and we use it as motivation and inspiration. Inherent by evolvement, betterment, and the laws of the universe tipping the axial with our super-powers of endless creativity and unity.

It's a huge difference between good and great. Nipsey's transition to the top was different from other people coming from similar space and background representing the struggle. Nipsey wanted others to be at the top, too. He helped people build things to create for themselves to develop their own roadmap to peak success. Which is their apex to the top. He showed us reverse engineering, starting from beginning to bite-size steps of how to grind it out slowly one step and day at a time. Which practice plans and further imprint a marathon effect.

Nipsey wasn't just a great artist, CEO, leader, and influencer. He was a great father, too. He mentioned his daughter and son in his records often. The best storytellers win and he moved you through his life stories and personal struggles, which moved people to be better fathers and engage more with parenthood and education for your children that school don't teach. Nipsey shared that and showed us the importance of doing more for each other and showing your kids and youth they can do more and truly create their dream into reality.

Every day is a challenge to create a masterpiece. You can't have a perfect day without finding someone and giving them something or doing something positive and uplifting for them. A gesture, an acknowledgement, some great advice, or simply listening to them. It don't have to be money. All you have to do is share your positive energy just like Nipsey did. Even though you may not have Nip's skill set of gravitating people to you, still be the best you in good faith to others.

It's about charity. Nipsey recognized his blessings and shared them wholeheartedly and without worrying about it coming back, selfless. Which it came back 1000x fold in abundance making him truly prolific. He was on the consistent pursuit of greatness. His best gift of telling a story in such an amazing relatable capturing way that the world felt it deeply. Most of all we knew he spoke truth and pushed the vibrant energy. He wasn't about individualism. He was about the people and betterment with novelty, risk-taking for ventures that outweighed the award. Dedication, inspiration, motivation.

- Chapter 2 -

"Incarcerated Lives Matter"

#IncarceratedLivesMatter. Some people would laugh. However, Nipsey Hussle knew this statement is true and incarcerated lives do matter. That it wasn't a laughing matter. From his luvıs to community and dayıs incarcerated. Also buying his music, book, and streaming all his works. The *Crenshaw, Marathon*, and *Victory Lap* was all in heavy rotation throughout the nation of massive incarceration chambers, state and federal facilities. Including women facilities.

It's over 2.5 million Afro-Americans incarcerated, with a lot of injustice, inequality, racial profiling, and simple probation violations. The list is exclusive and ongoing, which leads to an overcrowded prison population of massive black incarceration. There is definitely a bias and the penal system is broken, which Nipsey would contest of this and so many people lost in the system and families broken by the system. It wasn't rehabilitating, reentry programs valid for people reintegrating back into society.

The 13th Amendment of the United States Constitution states it shall abolish slavery except for a person being held for imprisonment by the government. Therefore it clearly says we all are modern-day black men enslavement by the government in every county, state, and federal institution of incarceration. Nipsey also knew this lies dormant in our U.S. Constitution Amendments. That the majority of our urban society forgets about.

It's a grand total of 6.7 million in the justice system including people incarcerated for technical violation. It's 80 billion on corrections annually, which they have private-owned correctional facilities and stock on corrections that shareholders consist of judges, lawmakers, House of Congress, lawyers, and law enforcement agencies. It's more prisons being built and funded versus schools and education funded programs. Nipsey also knew the statistics behind this, too, and implemented his own school funding program V-School to help with science research for kids.

"I want my actions to speak for me. I once read this book and his action spoke volumes while he was in silence in the room." Nipsey Hussle—B.E.T. interview

Once the details got rang out about how Nipsey Hussle was murdered helping a Luv1 fresh out reintegrate...we set this bitch on fire, rattling bars and kicking up helluva noise, irate and crushed! Affiliated and non-affiliated. The Crips nationwide was crushed. It felt like a spit in the face and a kick in the gut. Literally gasping, shaking our heads, mad as fuck.

Nipsey was the face of it and reintegrating people back into society without casting judgment. We couldn't pay our respects, be heard, and shine his inside influence and wave of love, too. We couldn't make our contribution how he was a symbol of storytelling thru his music all relatable subjects, his inspiration, motivation, and helluva influence.

Nipsey Hussle's music had substance unlike most club rap babbling today. His message was real, raw, and uncut with no caps. All factual and the Penn went loco and loved it. We finally had someone to tell our story and be the voice of us and the struggle and parallel confinements.

"Around the City it gotta be Cuhz, for the pieces I took off the Monopoly board." Nipsey Hussle—*Victory Lap*

Nip's music influenced us, moved us, inspired us, motivated us, dedicated us. Seeing if he can do it, then it's hope for us. We can follow his path or create our own routes and collaborate with all angles.

Each song and music has its own story, melody, ring, lyrics to enlighten mood. And most of all relatable, uplifting, and therapeutic. It took you there or back to a certain place.

Even from slavery fields, chain gangs, dated back to Africa songs and chants were made thru hardship. From villages, to warriors, and children of starvation. All use a rhythmic tone, the art of storytelling to stimulate the mind and touch their spirit and soothe their distress or emotional distress. Especially the loved ones entombed in these concrete and bar-caged tomb entities.

Being incarcerated makes you anti-social, self-centered, and isolated. Creates diminishing existence from society and forcibly alienate yourself. A left-in-the-dust and behind. Not everyone in jail is sex offenders or did heinous acts that deserve to be inside. Most of us suffer from harsh sentences, stiff guideline laws, unable to obtain proper representation nor due process. No voice and entrapment frustrated.

People lose sense of connection when they locked up and away from loved ones and society. Also sensibility further alienating themselves.

Jail calls, visits, emotional and family support and engagement matters. Which nowadays people lose contact with loved ones inside and don't really write or busy with their own lives and simply don't have time. However, no excuses with new innovated ways to connect with your loved ones on the inside. You can Google different ways and apps to connect. Some text message services to letters like textbehind.com. Or some you can send text and pics from your mobile device and it will go directly to the loved one incarcerated like pelipost.com. Both you can find in the app store. A little love goes a long way and would brighten someone's day or help reform their insight. Growth is innate and part of human nature.

"When I got out the county jail I heard myself on the radio. It sounded even better and it wasn't no turning back." Nipsey Hussle—radio interview

Ten years later Nipsey Hussle was nominated for a Grammy for Best Rap Album. Sitting front row with a tuxedo on and Lauren London accompanied arm-sided of him. In 2019 for his *Victory Lap* album released in 2018. The whole locked-down society was watching in awe, proud as hell. It was one of ours and the street people's champ.

Nipsey was in the county jail fighting a case from going to the joint and won his battle and came home. However, it was in that troubling time in the notorious L.A. County Jail which was gangbang central he validated himself and his time to do what he was meant to. Which upon his release he went harder with his music and created his platform and solidifying his own record label independent, doing it all with his own rights, masters, and merch. Branding himself creating and imprinting his Marathon in his own lane. Nipsey did get a taste of the county but it was pivotal to his transitional breakthrough. He looked at what his gifts, talents were. His strengths and weakness to discover his greatness. He seen negative people measure your possibilities based on their failures and they always too toxic. Detoxify your life. We surrounded by too many negative draining people so you can't reach your goals. Nip discovered this, too. He monitored his mind, watching the content he put in it and built with reading, learning, and education. Renewal of his mind and stayed self-discipline.

"Dats how you start off a curb server and end up a boss." Nipsey Hussle—*Victory Lap*

He knew his network will determine his net worth. Especially with all the half-ass content created globally from artist to filmmaker and online influencers. So he created a base, challenged himself and grew. It's a process of momentum. You must be willing to do what most people won't do or go. Kick it up a notch, high energy, and quantity with quality of service.

Nipsey created a diamond effect out of his pressure in the county jail during that court legal battle. He didn't stress out. He poked his chest out. He knew if he made his time work for him, not against him, he will create his own space. Making himself timeless. He'll have a millennia effect and his value will be priceless.

"Don't I take my time and take my tribe." Nipsey Hussle—*Victory Lap*

Prime example Nelson Mandela did the same with after 27 years of incarceration during a military militia in Africa. He got out to lead his people and of incarceration and shocked the world. He lived to the age of 95, which some people that didn't do 27 years in prison or time at all he outlived the most people nowadays. Till this day in Africa they still celebrate the life of Nelson Mandela and his birthday.

Also Stanley "Tookie" Williams, one of the Crip co-founders who was on death row in California, who was also self-reforming and educating. Using his time in that small cell all day for him writing books and kids' books. He was even nominated for a Nobel Peace Prize. Also used all his influence to self-help others and encourage them if they were smart enough to join a gang, be smart enough to rise above it. Despite the shift of Tookie's growth and positive energy after protest and celebrities like Snoop Dogg and Jamie Fox fighting for Tookie Williams to be pardoned, Arnold Schwarzenegger, the California governor at the time, refused to. After the pardon wasn't excused Stanley "Tookie" Williams was executed by lethal injection in California Dept. of Corrections.

Nipsey came with power from his platform and enabled us inside to tap in. We need some mentoring and coaching. Exercise our mind to discover what we great at.

"I been self-made from the dribble, I been saying I'ma killa." Nipsey Hussle—*Victory Lap*

We was on a level 4 watching T.V. and was tuned in to TMZ with a time caption slot that read: *Rapper Nipsey Hussle slaps press,* when they played the video and audio of Nipsey slapping the spit out of the cameraman that was pushed up on his bodyguard and taunting him.

We was lit and all laughing hard because we seen Nip was still hood as fuck and money didn't change him. Which we further loved and identified and respected. Nipsey Hussle was definitely one of ours, LOL. He can relate. Tupac said you can take a nigga out the hood, but not the hood out the nigga. This was facts. I had to take a smoke break that day with the fellas laughing and vibing to Nipsey Hussle's *Crenshaw* CD. That highlight was the topic trending inside for a week straight. It was all love. In such a serious hostile intense place, we all need a great laugh because we rarely smile. It's not a joking and laughing matter. Nip always brought light and life to the inside for us.

Nipsey seen in people what they didn't see in themselves. Blinded by opportunity. Negative is things you see and not focus on your goals because negativity consumes you and blurs your vision boards.

It's not what you leave for people, it's what you leave in them. Nipsey left a lot in us and empowered us to push ourselves, utilize time to work for us to yield harvest fruit after the germination processing of time in a marathon nonstop pace.

Nip was great at intellectual mastery of his time and space to create tenfold, especially during adverse times and harsh conditions. He also had a way for us to connect because he knew the struggle, pain, and what it was like to be caged with rage on the inside.

People need rehab or help. Love and support thru their growth process of darkness. Not prison. Every seed that's planted has to go thru an initial inception or germination process where it's dark, cold, and drowned out from outside elements before it arises, grows, or sprouts into greatness like Nipsey Hussle processed thru. People need support during their seed round.

We must take simple steps first to aid us in our growth process. Like build on black roots and have some appreciation of self. Self-worth and love thyself. Learn self, self-betterment, and self-help books. How-to books, or Google what you don't know and want or need to consume.

You are what you eat, drink, breathe, and think. Guard your mind and discipline yourself to stay focused on goal or master plan, movement, etc. Associate with positive people. Increase healthier relationships and eating habits which need to change, and recognize the detrimental of fast food, junk food, high salt, and excessive sugar intakes. It's pushing us African Americans with high blood pressure, heart disease, and diabetes. Must be conscious, bring awareness, spread words, and really imply it.

Outcries to the community and a supportive nature form. Reforming one step at a time.

It should be people and advocates with a solution and a few different bills, and start challenging more statutes and laws that's contributing to massive incarceration to biased broken judicial system.

Massive incarceration don't have no voice or platforms to be heard or helped.

Van Jones started a remediation project. He is an attorney, activist, and founder of 50 for prisoners. He says it's diamonds behind them walls and some starting to shine. I agree and we can all see what diamond it made with Nipsey Hussle. Even when they attempted to dim his light, he still shining even brighter. That's for sure, and the whole world can still see it like the superstar he was.

Now it's beginning to be a snowball effect with prison reform assistance from the outside reaching in to help free people of inequality and miscarriages of justice due to ample reasons including underlined flagrant bias. Now including a long list of influencers and celebrities, which is the voice, leverage, and spotlight norm people don't have. Especially living under the poverty line.

Like artist and reform activist Meek Mill and Jay Z, Kim K and co-founder Brittany K. Barnett, which Brittany Barnett helped directly impacted people to get home. She freed 17 people in 90 days, elevated their voices and helped reentry into society. I loved what Brittany said that she is picking locks on human cages.

Influencer is going all the way to the White House to state claims to the President. Recently influenced the President to reach out to Sweden to free ASAP Rocky.

Co-Chair Reform Alliance with Meek Mill pushed his lawyer finally got his bias case thrown out after 11 years and multiple violations and incarceration just because of his wealth and influence over his music. The judge showed bias. And she was black. You can't help but to shake your head and question how much of a broken system and problem we have with equality as black people in the world.

"You can never relate." Nipsey Hussle

I took the initiative to write this for Nipsey and everyone in locked-down society who can't speak out and to enlighten them not to fold. Hold on strong and seek knowledge and self-betterment. United we stronger, just like the Crips and Bloods coming more together in L.A. after Nipsey Hussle's passing. Nipsey even was to meet with police chief for gang violence prevention. He had that much influence. They went from trying to arrest him out of the same Marathon lot he ended up owning to them asking him for solutions.

Nipsey would have encouraged me to tell the truth and write the story and make sure it will be heard. He loved real and embraced the truth.

"Until we created equal—You'll never be my people." Nipsey Hussle

#IncarceratedLivesMatter #TheMarathonContinues

"Fades in the county jail. You could pull my file ya self." Nipsey Hussle—*Victory Lap*

- Chapter 3 -

"Prolific"

"I'm prolific so gifted." Nipsey Hussle—*Victory Lap*

Nipsey was Mr. Prolific. He owned it in every essence of it. He was a prolific artist, storyteller, and writer.

He tatted "Prolific" on the side of his face. However, he didn't have to tatt "Prolific" for you to see it. It showed in everything he did.

Nip was a prolific entrepreneur, prolific innovator, prolific visionary and creator. His music alone was prolific, but Nipsey's prolific was versatile.

Pro·lif·ic – adj: producing young or fruit abundantly 2: marked by abundant inventiveness or productivity. As defined in the *Merriam-Webster Dictionary* last time I checked.

Whereas Nipsey Hussle excelled the definition by notches. They may have to redefine the terminology after Nip because he was beyond abundant in inventiveness or productivity. Nip was working circles around prolific Fortune 500 and venture capital firms that had board of executives that graduated from top Ivy Leagues. However, they still couldn't match Nipsey's prolific mind state, light-years ahead. The board of 12 executive members was watching Nipsey's moves. He had his own cryptocurrency and planned to make it affordable for everyone, especially in the hood. Five more years from now it wouldn't been no stopping Nipsey Hussle. He would own half of L.A. and on his way to be a billionaire. That's facts.

Nipsey had a prolific résumé that was impeccable. He had 14 different businesses, real estate, author, vest and follow coin, Vector 90, teacher, radical entrepreneur, activist, philanthropist, CEO, brand, humanitarian, revolutionary, reforming prisoners reintegrating, advocate, signed deal with Puma, Def Jam. Donate thousands to schools. Funding science school programs. Working with the homeless, feeding, clothing, and employing them. Most of all, fixed up his Crenshaw district and brought his community up positive with jobs created for them. Started movements to unite and stop the black-on-black violence.

Now that's just a brief of some of Nipsey's prolific résumé. It's a lot more out there you can research online to see in finer details. Nobody couldn't emulate that or how Nipsey multiplied and morphed his time. And what's such a success story about Nipsey Hussle was he started off broke and made something out of nothing growing up in the worst section of the gangland murder capital and birthplace. Nipsey's father was an Eritrean immigrant from Africa. He wasn't born with a silver spoon in his mouth or left a family inheritance and business to capitalize and monopolize. Like most of us, he didn't have a head start at life. He started out in the negative and had to overcome a lot of obstacles and rise above a lot of hurdles of negativity in a toxic environment. This is why he is the people's champ.

Nipsey Hussle's legacy, ideas, independent label, connection, evolution, design, art forms, clothing, community engagement, his words, lyrics, principles, elements, sustainability, intellectual properties, license to manufacture was timeless and his prolific continues to relay into a marathon with a peculiar pace.

"I'd tell you to live your life and grow." Nipsey Hussle—*Victory Lap*

Nipsey was the one that made it out and it was so prolific and legendary. Only one makes it out, the rest of us end up in locked-down society or double-stacked graves in the cemeteries with county burials because 87 percent of us in the urban communities don't have insurance policy plans.

"Million-dollar policy on my flesh, nigga, I am nothin like you other rap niggas." Nipsey Hussle—*Victory Lap*

When you sit and watch Nipsey Hussle videos, interviews, or at the Grammys, he was always authentic. He didn't try to be prolific; he was. Most people have to try and maintain a visual image of their lyrics or fake reality of entertainment. People will do anything to stay in that number-one spotlight, even if it's a gimmick. And we never seen a prolific gimmick. Nipsey was a genius and mastermind in all aspects. I'd see people with cartoons or their names on their chains. Nipsey had Malcolm X famous pic with Malcolm's chin resting on his fist in solid gold and diamonds on his chain. It was a statement and everyone that knew Malcolm X history of his radical reform process once he went to God, Islam, and self-educated himself.

Nipsey wasn't like the rest and his amplitude of prolificness was the best. He beat all odds and wasn't just a prolific artist. He was more than just rap and his legacy and blueprint he left showed that.

"I ain't always been pious and have it like that. I ain't quit. I went thru every emotion." Nipsey Hussle—*Outro*

The fact that Nipsey overcame his situation but didn't denounce his background and people resonated his path even more. Defeating obstacles of the human emotions we all have and battle. Also the more money, the more problems like Biggie Smalls rapped about. Even a lot of world-famous celebrities committed suicide time and time over again. Because their emotional state isn't right. If you a billionaire, you wealthy and can feed a continent and buy private islands and jets. However, if you're not rich in spirit and wealthy mentally, you will be a mess. Like attempting to run a marathon after a junk food and caffeine binge. Or running a marathon without no proper stretching. Your mind and body must be whole and in tune, else you will be a wreck in distress of an emotional breakdown and be more subjectable to negativity that pulls your emotion state into real feelings, which leads to manifesting internal distress of your physical, not just mental no more. You can get high blood pressure, strokes, heart attack, etc. You have to let go of negative emotion and don't let them accumulate until it physically pulls you down.

Nipsey mastered his by putting them in check. Simple hacks only temporarily work. You must acknowledge it and ignore or redefine it. Be very thankful and appreciative. Gratitude for your heart beating and you still breathing. Whatever your ideal hardship or situation isn't going to kill you. It builds you up for success and everything you trying to achieve just as Nipsey followed his. If it's negative people hating or criticism, simply remove yourself and elevate with surrounding yourself around better positive uplifting people. Most of all, it starts with self-belief and structure of processing your emotion state of mind.

Most people want to run a marathon but under 4 minutes. They want to be seen first at 1st place and compete with all the other contestants. It don't mean you're not number 1 or don't possess the qualities of a number 1 contender. Most people have a rigid idea of what they supposed to have entitlement. Thinking they are prolific and the world supposed to hand them everything instantly without being devoted or putting in the intense work of reputation. Your entire life you will never have true control. You will have the illusion of control. You set goals and succeed, so you think you have control and also see others do it and reach their goals, too.

In reality, any of the thousands of things to deter you from the goals could have prevented your path and derailed it further off course. It's true you can create a clear path or destiny. However, you can't control its outcome. It's unpredictable and many twists and turns plus falling spiral spins. It's the internal monologue in your head. And the mental model of this the way the world works. Then you'll start getting confirmation around you because you believe it's how the world works. Just like the universal laws of attraction, or like when you a baby and think you in control over everything in your life but you constantly need your mother and multiple elements. Even after you grow into adulthood, you still think that you can control everything in your universe, but that's not reality. You have to know, learn and let go of things you can't control. And this is what Nipsey shared he conquered.

"Pop clutch switch lanes on you niggas." Nipsey Hussle—*Victory Lap*

Nipsey Hussle was a prolific author of his *Marathon* book, where he breaks down his logic, mental, methodology of teaching and completed business framework. Created transformation. The value benefit, or end result you want to create. Especially his empowerment and innovation. Nip's intellect was brilliant to be a self-educated inner-city young black man underprivileged with only self-seeking tools of knowledge. I was proud some will be amazed. It shows his growth and development with a helluva blueprint. *The Marathon* is a must-read for everyone self-building and reforming. It gives you a clear state of Nip's mind and vision that came into existing. Again, straight prolific writer, which I give it 5 stars because I love perpetual progress, mentorship, and betterment. Plus it came from Nip's works of many arts we love.

"Ya Dad gone, let me be ya Daddy. We both come from broken families." Nipsey Hussle—*Crenshaw*

Quitters never win...and winners never quit. Facts. Some say entrepreneurs are taught and you can learn any skill set. I say true entrepreneurs are born naturally gifted with a Type-A entrepreneurial adoptive mindset. Some build themselves as a brand, market their message, specialize in niche expertise, with persistence, creative productivity. Fearless, management/leadership skills, risk takers, and crush expectations. They stay lit with passion, motivation, and inspiration. They refuse to stop until they prevail with task, project, vision, movement or innovation.

"Don't I take my time and take my tribe." Nipsey Hussle—*Victory Lap*

Nipsey had prolific principles and left them imprinted all around L.A. and stamped on his music. That night when me and the fellas put one in the air for Nip after he made TMZ headliner for slapping dude and protecting his tribe always, we was streaming *Victory Lap*. How Nip's words saturate your mind and was pleasant to your ears. They say what you love to hear is called music to your ears. As I exhaled the smoke out my nostrils like a Chicago bull, it wasn't the only thing that consumed my mind. Nipsey's sound and words played into a huge factor. His lyrics you paid attention to because you know is real because you lived it before or been down a similar path. It was a proud grin to see Nipsey win. A Crip win and rep for lockdown society and the streets.

It was just something authentic the way Nip said those words that you felt and he truly owned it. Was Nipsey Hussle the great prolific. It still hit me when I hear that *Victory Lap* and him spit it.

"I'm prolific so gifted." Nipsey Hussle—*Victory Lap*

"I take the stance and willing to die for it." Nipsey Hussle

- Chapter 4 -

"Nip's Influence"

"I'm Nipsey Hussle—check me out, made my money double—check me out." Nipsey Hussle—*Marathon*

Nipsey's influence was dynamic globally. He was far different from a social media influencer. Nip was an influencer over 3 different generations. His city, coast, neighborhood, and lockdown society he had influence and was the face of it. His influence was a concoction of various qualities, passionate about helping and building his community, educating the youth and people, helping people from the heart just to touch them enough to smile. His influence was empowerment.

The most influential was his music. We've seen how Nip kept it hood with his lyrics, tatts, and apparel. Then he had unique sound with a Cali blend of culture and beats. It was always right sound and Nipsey's flow was so authentic how he delivered his bars and hooks. Also his exclusive punchlines.

"These niggas is Hollyweird." Nipsey Hussle

"And Loc out in Vegas, didn't we cream puff them punks—50¢ and Mayweather fleed the scene with us...True story." Nipsey Hussle—*Grinding All My Life*

His music had an effect on us who can relate and move to it. Women and kids even parents loved when the Nipsey Hussle video would come on. His music began to evolve with a mogul sound of greatness. *Victory Lap* was the perfect timing. Nipsey chop-n-pop, gassin flames, and versatile was mastered in all levels. A music genius creating different songs.

When I called my N-Hood cuzo Tucca he said, "Cuhz out here riding around Compton in a Brinks truck." Then the whole level 4 yard was trending with Nip pulling up in an armored truck. This was helluva influence without no negative energy, and people was truly inspired and excited. I must have read 10 different business proposals and heard literally 5 or 6 albums written by different inspiring rappers thru their reform to hit big like Nip was driving around in armored vehicles.

"All money in—no money out!" Nipsey Hussle—*Marathon*

That was the movement, not just the motto. Nipsey had the whole world buzzing with all money in! He taught people how to stack in an urbanized way. From a consumer to a conserver. Economizing smart with a subconscious methodology to it. It made you seriously think before you just spend and shell out your money on new things in the marketplace simply because you see it. When in reality, you fine and don't actually need it because you still breathing, healthy, and saving up to invest or for your goal and rainy days of emergency. Plus you or loved ones' education.

Nipsey's mastery of his mind influence first before he can project it into the world. His right vocals, videos, clothing, brand, and creating his platform and household name. Your mind has to be influenced to create your visionary process. In order to dominate your mind, you must inherent your innate influence to perpetuate your visions into existence. Automate it directly into a sure reality. This will further push you to have better influence over your life and decision making to make the impossible very possible.

"Summer time in my Cutlass." Nipsey Hussle—*Crenshaw*

My favorite Nipsey Hussle albums are *Crenshaw*, *Marathon*, and *Victory Lap*, in that order, which all influenced me to do a 180-degree straight turnaround in my reform and growth and development mind cocoon. Nipsey's music influenced me to start using my time for me vs. against me, which I started telling people incarcerated how to self-heal and build to soul search and find their own blueprint like their own unique thumbprint. Plus we was all listening to 2 of Nip's CDs, *Crenshaw* and *Marathon*, at the time to help influence us to push the positive energy and break out our bad impulsive habits.

The *Crenshaw* album cover was dope of Nipsey with the hat and the braids with his arms folded fly as ever. The facial tatts was the most influential, especially that money sign S because

Nipsey didn't just tatt it, he owned it, too. He didn't have to tatt it to know he was about his money. When Nipsey was 18 he had an all-white Lincoln on chrome wheels sitting very clean and slick.

Nip's influence on just a CD cover alone had everyone tatting money signs on their face. Even though it's part of our culture nowadays, it's not so much taboo anymore.

"I'm self-made—I made myself." Nipsey Hussle—*Victory Lap*

That statement had influenced us to say it did not matter about our felony prior convictions or our tatts on our face. We would all take on as self-made influencers creating ourselves entrepreneurs. However, I'm not recommending you tatt yourself up and think you going to grow rich and not ever work again. You must self-educate marketing, planning strategies, innovation, and creative content that you can add value and scale it. It's not an easy path. Nipsey influenced us to start our initial self-growth process of education and all money in.

"Never been out of town with a trunk full of pounds in a .38 with a I-gotta-get-it type urgency." Nipsey—*Marathon*

When Nipsey did his B.E.T. interview, he would talk about the book influences on his life. Reading was essential for him and it was knowledge to feed his innovation. He would always encourage people to read. He mentioned a book that talked about actions done in silence without being seen. And he wanted it to be the name of his last album he released and his motive behind his movement.

Each interview Nipsey spoke with intellect and it made you be attentive with every word to soak up game. I think this was one of his greatest attributes and most definitely influential.

"Take you out back, let you expose ya rage, take you across the track, let you explode a face...you official now." Nipsey Hussle— *Victory Lap*

Nipsey was born August 15th. He was a Leo and a straight lion. Some don't believe the zodiac constellation in astrology or Mercury retrograde. I think some people act similar to their zodiac signs born under. The proof is in the person. If Nipsey didn't stroll like a lion, roar like a lion, and eat like a lion or take care of his pride inside his kingdom like a lion, he wouldn't have been born under the Leo sign. Nip always been aligned with the stars bright and high in the cosmos and astrological universe.

I think it's super intriguing how it shows and outlines Nip's influential algorithm in astrology. By definition, As·trol·o·gy – noun: Divination based on the supposed influence of the stars upon human events. Facts!

"Where ya code at, niggas die every day, can't control that." Nipsey Hussle

Nipsey's influence was so evident that he was supposed to meet up with police chief a day after he got murdered to discuss gang violence prevention. So he definitely was the face of it, too. Nipsey said people die every day but you can't control that. However, the police chief and gang task force felt Nip actually could help prevent it from his influence and the fact he had a solution with a proper format. Mostly because he had influence on other gangs and neighborhoods outside of his. Nipsey had respect, not just clout. When an individual is well respected for his good deeds, leadership, and as an example of a role model and success story, it demands the utmost respect, not attention. Compton is gang central, so they knew how Nipsey and Y.G. came together and without no tragedy or incidents. Besides the police shutting down the Fuck Donald Trump video shoot.

"Protest is important...I think Y.G. is a musical genius..." Nipsey Hussle

Even though Nipsey passed away, that didn't stop his acquaintance from meeting with the police chief to discuss strategies and coming up with prevention resolutions. All lives matter, and I think it starts with redirecting the attention and focus to positive and more structural social behaviors and role models for the youth. Youths usually start often with behavior problems, gateway drugs, and violence due to broken families of absence of parents or neglect. Some motives are money or protections by their peers. Others join the gangs because it's a norm now of the follower effect. Parents are either incarcerated or addicted to drugs and alcohol which force too many youth to be street influenced, misled further into more toxic environments that's hard to make it out and eventually lead to prison or an early grave. Most don't have a lot of outlets and opportunities. I think it starts with positive influences on our youth and taking responsibility in our own communities to inspire, lead, heal and self-betterment. One person and day at a time. Spreading self-awareness is key.

"I think our reaction to being disrespected, we need to reevaluate that and work on it." Nipsey Hussle

Once everyone seen Nipsey's influence over gang prevention, it signified his status of a community leader. Because not every rapper in the industry had true influence past the culture influence of their music. Not their community or as a person outside of being an actual artist.

You don't see a lot of young artists—or artists, period—giving back to their very own communities nor building them up. Feeding the homeless, building jobs and creating opportunities. All Nipsey's contributions to school, youth, and research is what moves us the most. You can't be a helluva influencer all around like Nip if you selfish and all about self-gain. Nipsey Hussle was selfless, which I think more of us need to adopt this type behavior and follow the trend.

"Ocean views, small circle, chosen few." Nipsey Hussle—*Victory Lap*

Nipsey had a small circle but a big network that influenced the whole world to follow and take note of. It spoke volumes.

"First get the money and respect. Then the power come next." Nipsey Hussle—*Victory Lap*

People try to see how Nipsey did it to be successful and relevant plus a real influencer from the hood. You cannot duplicate authentication. Nip started with his environment and used all his natural hood and street elements like a poetry. Nip mastered the art of storytelling, except his wasn't the average fictional tale. His was a reality show of real events and timelines of his life with no extra fictitious scenes. Just raw and uncut. All of us love true stories with an epic ending. Nipsey should have been put on *TIME* for the most influential people, not just nominated. Facts. I loved the facts he used his surrounding and neighborhood to make something out of nothin into gold.

- Chapter 5 -

"Nip's Impact"

"Streets voice out west, self-made legendary progress." Nipsey Hussle—*Victory Lap*

Nip's impact was global and multicultural. He had a vibing impact with his music, clothing, and movement. It wasn't no valuation that could be put on Nip's impact. It's priceless. His human resources and engagement were priceless. We all start out equal. Most people never know their full potential or see their dreams come into existence, which dreams without goals are just dreams and cannot be achieved without discipline and consistency. This is why Nip's impact is still to this day as you read this still relevant and ongoing. The whole world saying the marathon continues and all money in!

You have to find what you love and love what you do. Your work will be great. Nipsey loved his community and hood and took them on his back to the top with him and all around him. His impact was on millions of people internationally. From him dreaming big going outside the box and think outside of the box. He planned and worked at his goals and craft daily.

Blacc Sam, Nip's big bro, said Nipsey had a natural talented gift of rapping and being self-taught. He built his own computer with different computer parts one-by-one, little-by-little. Then one day he came home and Nip had the whole computer built all by himself.

Nipsey was committed and persistent and did whatever it takes to complete and prime his brain. This connects your vision to your brain into reality. This was a most crucial important to his life impact and blueprint. His basic principle was to achieve excellence in his life endeavors. His developing principles of love, elevation, goal-setting.

His brain was just like the computer he was building. The same electricity generated with movement and interaction. All of our neurons are electrified with signals specialized processing of fundamental functions of the nervous system. In actuality, computer science and neuroscience are synonymous with lightning speed of electronic functions and systematic.

I think Nip's impact will be a definite everlasting effect because you couldn't crowd-source it or relate it to anybody else's blueprint. Everyone has their own unique impact. All you can do is sit in awe looking at Nipsey's.

"Double up, triple up, banged on the whole gang. I didn't give a fucc." Nipsey Hussle—*Victory Lap*

Nipsey was already in motion to get light rail train to run down through the Crenshaw district passing the Marathon Clothing store and Slauson Ave. Now his impact for the train down Crenshaw is coming to existence.

It's also a petition in circulation for Nipsey Hussle's own street. I think that's a major blessing and accomplishment. We was all proud and lit in locked-down society to hear that and Nipsey's name to be forever part of what he loved and was most adamant about his community.

He should definitely get a Hollywood star on the Walk of Fame with the iconic stars. Muhammad Ali, who was also a humanitarian, has a Hollywood star, too. However, Muhammad Ali's star isn't on the ground like Trump's. Instead, his is on the wall because he said he don't want no white man walking and stepping all over his name. You can't help but to salute that and what he stood for also.

I also think because of Nipsey's huge impact on West Coast culture and influence that he should have his own banner or jersey hanging up at the Staples Center as contribution to Nipsey Hussle's legacy and endorse him as a hometown hero and community activist in L.A. Mainly giving so much back to the community and bringing so much and such a big impact to the community.

Nip's impact was implemented into practice in so many regions. His naturalism, action, or thought based only on natural desires and instincts. He was a naturalistic with realism in his art and literature.

Nipsey also embodied Dr. Martin Luther King Jr.'s message behind his speech in the '60s. Dr. King stated: "Fly! If you can't fly, run! If you can't run, walk! If you can't walk, crawl! The objective is constant movement. It's the only way you'll find your true divine blueprint."

Most of us don't go back and study or read our history and learn about our ancestors and from them. Their systems implemented or their road maps. Sometimes even a lesson to be learned from their costly mistakes, good or bad.

However, this is what Nipsey did, was read, study, practice, and apply. Don't be afraid to innovate and reinvent the wheel. Your dreams and desire is all possible and could lead to be impactful, too eventually.

There has been over 107 billion people that lived on this Earth till this date and the beginning of humanity. Therefore, the dead outweigh the living 15 to 1. All what humanity done learned and evolved, or revolutionized from past timelines on discovered knowledge. Some people like Nipsey Hussle are so impactful it's a breakthrough, a change, move or advance and contribute to the world. Also rich cultural context and all great historians, creators, and artists.

When Nip stated he went thru every emotion, he also went thru every level of habits, too. Good and bad habits. It's little hacks to alter your habits but not to fix or master them how Nipsey explained. Your willpower needs to be tested around designed hard circumstances.

We must establish good habits before we can master desired goals. Society social norms have an inherent influence and expectations. Then we interpret cues and desired behavior of bad habit like everyone else's.

You must understand our habits are compound interest of choices we make. How Nipsey showed us habits that are immediately outcome is favorable vs. the long-term immediate gratification. Nipsey was big on taking his time to develop and embody his desired goals.

Each time you body writing, you establish yourself as a writer. Each behavior casts enough votes to the person you want to become. Habits desire the dream person you become.

Reading is a metahabit. If you find a great book, read it twice. Reading is very therapeutic and helps you learn anything possible. This is why Nipsey knew the essence of reading and expressed how vital it was to you.

If you don't rise to the levels of your goals, you still will fall in love with your new system. How long it takes to build a new habit? Some books and scholars say 66 days, others say 3 weeks depending if it's a bad or good habit and how heavy the habit is based and desired.

However, it will become automatic in time with my own personal experience. Everyone is different. Willpower is essential. You still need to put in your repetitions and practice. Then your brain will automate. You have to have awareness, then practice.

The way you develop expertise is writing about it daily. They say the dullest pencil is better than the sharpest mind. All great renowned geniuses since the beginning of time always had journals, notes, and writing things down. Nipsey embodied this, too, and naturally adoptive of this written pattern of the greats, which furthered his development further not just in music, but he became a great prolific writer. This tradition needs to be carried along with Nipsey's marathon continuance. It also shows why Nip owned it. Nipsey Hussle the Great!

How do you get started and motivated? Most books tell you why, but not how. How to implement what you're reading, to carry it out or put into practice. It's a motivation or reinforcement with most self-help books. It's steps to creating positive habits. 1st a cue, 2nd a craving, 3rd a response, and 4th a reward. You must use habits as small stepping stones to get to the next level.

Video games are examples of masters at habit formation. They all have reason of immediate satisfaction and progress. People love progress and will keep coming back.

Downscale any habit to fit in 2 minutes for 1st two weeks. First you got to just show up to start owning your desires before you can master it. You can join a group or a person where your desired behavior is a norm behavior, and you can apply this methodology so you can master your good habits into greatness and have a big impact on the world like Nipsey Hussle the Great mastered. I'm not saying it's easy to replicate; you must drop bad habits first and reverse practice into good habits.

"If it's not love, then it's looking like hate." Nipsey Hussle—*Marathon*

Nipsey was open to constructive criticism. He wanted to know the real and uncut truth. What the people, especially his fans and supporters, mattered most to Nip. It wasn't for validation, but to give us his best and being the best at his craft.

"When I was done with *Victory Lap* I took it to Puff and asked him to listen to it...Puff told me he wanted to hear that more West Coast stamp... So I went back and redid a few mix and masters, a few tweaks... But not the words cuz my lyrics was fine..." Nipsey Hussle—VL interview

I loved the fact that Nip's head wasn't too big for himself. Even though he was on top, he still was humble. And it showed. If it wasn't for him gathering people's opinions about his project, including Mogul Puffy, *Victory Lap* wouldn't be quite the masterpiece it is. Nipsey left us his finishing touches of his perfection. I think other people's impact had an overall impact on Nipsey, and this further aided his greatness and morphed him to a higher level of energy than the subconscious can fathom.

"Word from the set, we accept the challenge." Nipsey Hussle—*Victory Lap*

Nipsey also used his leverage to give others a chance to elevate and how to master the root of challenges. Every great leader or creator has real huge impacts to lead a nation and ability to problem solve to the world. Just like Nip's impressiveness.

Obama's impact and ability to connect with people and bring a new method and message to problem solving. The simple tagline, punchline, campaign slogan or whatever you prefer to call it, "It's time for a change," words from Obama was such music to the ears, soothing to the soul, and a sense of relief. That one line made Obama iconic and impactful enough to move the nation and voted him inside the Oval Office.

Nipsey had the same impact with his "All money in, no money out" slogan. Empowerment, self-awareness, growth, education, time management, and learning. Impressive and interesting people always leave impactful marks on this Earth.

Steve Jobs said he'd give up some of his billions to live another year after his battle with cancer before he passed.

Nipsey went on to open up a dialogue about health, too. He stated health is important and awareness that our brain forgets almost 90 percent of the things we study. We remember our social feeds and memes, but not enough about our health. We don't stay focused on it or food-conscious of what we poison our bodies with. Health is vital because without spiritual, physical, and mental health, you cannot push your fullest peak potential as ordained. Your energy will be off. It's like trying to dance if your mind is not in the mood. You won't move the same and have your top performance versus you being excited to dance and in a positive vibrant mood to dance. Then you will kill it and possibly go viral.

"Where ya hos at, what ya rolls at, where ya heart at, where ya day 1 niggas, where all them stories you telling, we will expose that, where ya backbone at." Nipsey Hussle

- Chapter 6 -

"Motivation"

"If the police get behind me, that's a car chase, looking back at my life make my heart race." Nipsey Hussle—*Victory Lap*

Nip's music was so powerful and motivation. It moved people. To sway their heads, dance, love, think, cry, work out, and grind it out. So much passion, realness, and relatable connections. The art of storytelling being composed on a motivational beat with a thump.

You ever see a level 4 180 rec yard full of Crips walkin, grooving, and sliding on cue synchronized like a swimmer? No, you can't Google that or have a GoPro on the inside. However, I can tell you and share with you that when Nipsey Hussle's music and hard hitting beats come on the playlist or T.V., especially that *Grinding All My Life*, it had Crips walkin light and swift on their tippy-toes drippy, moving abruptly side-to-side. The C.O.'s watch and glare but can't kill the vibe and wouldn't dare to interface.

I guess it was the laws of nature or some would say the laws of physics. They wouldn't budge as the Crips rejoiced to Nipsey

Hussle's legendary music. Nip's music connected and interlocked with us. It moved or inspired anyone who heard his back story and message. His motivational music even had people improvising and acting things out.

Locked-down society damn near riot when Nipsey Hussle didn't make the 2019 Top 10 list of best rappers ever. And Tupac came in at #15. We didn't know where they computed them algorithms from or what survey and poll that was based off of. Because the streets and locked-down society beg to differ.

"I'll say it again, bitch, I'm the man. Bitch, I'm the man!" Nipsey Hussle—*Marathon*

Nipsey's concerts was always off the charts. State-to-state he would bring the roof down, and a few concerts' aftermath led to shootings from people being too lit and pumped up so their same rivals were Nipsey fans and concertgoers and they would clash in a few incident around the country. The Crips and the Bloods all listened to Nipsey's music. Once Nipsey found out about the incidents and certain venues trying to ban him and his music, Nipsey spoke out against the violence, not condoning it. Nip's music is seen to them as a correlation, but it's not the sole blame of people being drunk and violent. It could be implied as a mere blame but isn't the main factor between people problems and ongoing fueled beefs. Nipsey was encouraging people to kill that beef and leave it at the door, and thinking about coming together to build for your family and communities.

"Keep the hood out your mouth, or you gotta be charged."
Nipsey Hussle—*Victory Lap*

Nipsey was also self-motivated. He made himself so he motivated his along with disciplining himself. In Nipsey's *Dedication* song, he said motivating hard work and dedication. He created value thru his community and society from his own experiences. He had to be motivated to turn a corner and rethink his angles to penetrate his goals, which pushed him straight to the Grammys' front row. Him being Grammy-nominated was motivated from *Victory Lap* that he perfected as his project passionate with hard work.

Nip had brought his loved ones with him to the Grammys. His homegirl day 1 Nuney Loc told Nip it didn't matter if he won or not cuz he was already a winner and won! She was 100 percent right and already motivated thru Nipsey's constant energy of empowerment.

Nipsey wasn't a motivation speaker like you see on YouTube or podcast, but when he spoke, it was motivation. How he constructed his words and said it in a poetic way and melody to open the spirit up by inspired lyrics. One of the greatest poets to perform and permeates motivation in your everyday life.

Nip was a musical mentor, too. It's hard when the industry and world lose artists, because great people don't grow on trees. It's a lost art of making state-of-the-art nowadays. Nip did a great helluva job in creating art, performing, motivating, and showing others to perfect their arts. Don't nobody want to put in the work or do a prestigious package and have that umph desire no more to create sound projects. It's been a lot of fast-track cliché rap on the radios lately.

Nipsey's process of creation was immaculate. Nip's sense of melody was unlike nobody else's and a hit maker. Nip's businesses was a vehicle for creation and how to maintain culture and speed. Also to act on a vision.

We hear his words and translate them to our own stories, meanings or reality experiences. He knew how to bridge that gap. He knew how to interpret our reality into storytelling composed medium to a unique direct path to people's emotions, senses, etc. Music matters a lot and guides you there. Composition is how you exist. You feel an emotion closeness to the music so you feel a physical closeness to the artist, life, and stories. All this was inspired by Nipsey's strong motivation and willpower.

He was great at rebranding himself not just as a narrative producer and director. He pushed beyond the screens and behind the scenes in his music medium. You need a specific person to do a specific job. Not everyone is qualified to get the quality job done right. You need a detailed plan backed by serious motivation, then overcome any and all standing obstacles like Nip did. Nipsey motivated and taught us to reinvest is key, thriving, and double money. Advising, investing, and building a great team to assist in goal or mission objective. A good idea, vision, or product and build a movement. Remember the two H's...Health and Happiness.

"Nobody trippin handle business got my digits up." Nipsey Hussle—*Victory Lap*

It was so many Nipsey Hussle tributes globally. Tribute videos and songs with different artists known and local showing Nip love and how he motivated and touched them, too. And millions of fans' social media *Rest in Peace Nipsey Hussle the Great* hashtags and posts of genuine love. His motivation, inspiration, and raw unfiltered realness will be greatly missed and appreciated.

People didn't embellish enough on Nipsey's fly-ass tuxedo he wore to the Grammys. That was fly as hell and motivated us in locked-down society with Nip coming straight out of Crenshaw and really being in them streets, from them streets, and about them streets in all fashions of aiding and assisting the community and youth. Plus we was laughing how low and red Nip's eyes were at the Grammys. It wasn't no secret and legal for recreational use in the state of California. It just don't get no more exclusive or better than that.

In June of 2018, the year before the Grammy nominee Nipsey Hussle made his B.E.T. debut, he performed at the B.E.T. Experience. Soon as that *Last Time I Checked* came on, it was so many Crips standing up in the T.V. room on the compound. The Locs started chucking up Crip signs and throwing up hand signs in a frenzy throughout the duration of Nipsey's whole B.E.T. performance. Nipsey's motivation brought light in some of the most dim places, and that music pushes us to want change, be better for our families and communities. We began to appreciate what you have in front of you, and understanding how difficult life or situations may seem, you don't give up and still have a chance and hope.

When we also seen Nip with the youth donating the $10,000 check and all the kids' smiling faces, it was a priceless pic. It was motivation because a lot of us have kids or younger siblings that we have influence over, and we want to connect with them to be better than us. Mainly push the importance of their education like Nipsey encouraged and promoted. I love to see people giving back and investing our youth. I believe our youth is the truth and they will inherit the future, but we must lead by great examples and step up our actions and mentorships. Nipsey's spirit will forever be blessed and shine for all his great contributions, especially into the youth of the communities. With all the student debt crisis and youth playing Fortnite or on their mobile devices all day and nite, they started to think people don't need college nowadays. They also have been influenced by social media platforms to think they can snap or stream live their own reality shows and will be discovered and famous after going into a viral sensation. Nipsey Hussle gets a triple salute for his youth movement, foundations, and donations to school funding and programs with no sweat wholeheartedly.

We can all connect with the youth and encourage them one-by-one. You don't have to be rich like Nip to do for kids and educating the youth. You can be rich in heart like Nip and use his road map as motivation to help and contribute to the youth in your communities. From backpack drives, supplies, after-school programs, coaching, encouraging to read books, starting youth foundation and movements, and getting people involved on your social outlets. It's plenty to be done. You don't need a building or money because it's endless opportunities and sponsorship programs and entities. Good faith, good means, and good willpower goes a long way. Also, seeds just need to be planted first and eventually they will grow. I believe that's the germination process of life and Nipsey exceeded and exemplified that to the fullest. I vow to do my contribution and continue Nip's Marathon blueprint he laid down by example by investing into our youth educations and future.

"They was selling Zips in the set, make a quarter mill—no sweat." Nipsey Hussle—*Victory Lap*

Four months after Nipsey Hussle's passing, *The New York Times* reported and exposed Los Angeles Police Department having Nipsey Hussle as the head of their investigation of his shopping plaza and the Marathon Clothing store for continuous criminal activity in the shopping plaza.

The Los Angeles P.D. denied it and all allegations of investigating Nipsey and property. Then a few weeks later, the City of Los Angeles sent a notice to his shopping plaza, challenging them to clean up or move out, listing it was a hotbed for continuous criminal activity, even though the Marathon Clothing store had been closed down.

It's still ongoing controversy with L.A.P.D. and Nipsey's shopping plaza. It's like a spit into the community and fans' faces because Nipsey was an activist and community leader, and the police chief went to him for gang prevention. He was an advocate and I was motivated to write about all Nipsey's positive contributions, influence, arts, life, and community activist and reform advocate, etc. Not the hate.

- Chapter 7 -

"Epic Funeral (Homecoming)"

"How you die thirty-something after all these years bangin?"
Nipsey Hussle—*Victory Lap*

Rest in Peace Ermias "Nipsey Hussle" Asghedom, 8/15/85 to 3/31/19 Homecoming. Nipsey's Homecoming service of celebrating his life, arts, and legacy was epic! His Homecoming took place in the L.A. Staples Center. It was only one funeral held there prior to Nip, and that was Michael Jackson, the King of Pop. So that only means it's fair to say Nipsey was the King of Rap. The whole Staples Center was jammed to capacity with family, friends, fans, celebrities, loved ones, and the supporting community.

Once everyone in locked-down society receive the news that Nip's funeral won't be televised for the people that couldn't make it to L.A. to pay respects, it was an uproar for a few days. Until we found out that Jay-Z was streaming the services thru Tidal platform. We was highly grateful because when we touched down, we can always go back and stream it ourselves. Shortly after we found out even better news that on local cable, B.E.T. was airing

Nip's Homecoming live uninterrupted. It was a huge sigh of relief. Especially how much Nipsey had an impact on prison reform and how much locked-down society loved Nip and his music. It was a lot of thug tears shed that day just from the true genuine love Nipsey showed and shared. He was our street success story and voice of the streets and sweltering with the heat of injustice and oppression in the penal system. It was bittersweet. We just really appreciated Nip putting us in history, being a voice for us in the struggle, and not forgetting about us believing second chance to reform and doing 180-degree turnarounds for betterment.

"She say you probably die alone, I say you probably right." Nipsey Hussle—*Victory Lap*

Nipsey Hussle's Homecoming eulogy was fly. It had a pic of Nip in white suit, hair braided back with some wing consuming the sky-blue skyline background.

The service was opened up with an epic written letter from former President Barack Obama. Nipsey's loved one read the prestigious letter of acknowledgement. She went on to state that Obama sent his regards to Nip's kids, family, and Lauren London. Obama acknowledged Nipsey for being a community advocate and overcoming adversity and prospering. He also stated he didn't know Nipsey Hussle, but his daughters knew his music and were fans, too. This was very exclusive and had people in locked-down society standing up out their seats, especially when

Obama acknowledged Nip's big impact and contributions to the community and youth.

Next, the Honorable Minister Louis Farrakhan came in state to attend Nipsey's Homecoming and delivered his speech with the Nation of Islam. Farrakhan's sermon he shared a testimony he had on his way to the Staples Center about Nipsey Hussle and the bird that traveled thousands of miles from Southern California to south of the border every year and back. He explained the small bird having red on its head and blue on his chest. How it reminded him of Nipsey's influence on the Crips and the Bloods of coming together and uniting for positive change and being pillars of the community. Farrakhan was an immaculate inspiring motivational speaker that spoke with so much regard and pious. It was epic and he told us to follow Nipsey's greatness path and better self by stopping black-on-black violence in our own communities.

Stevie Wonder was playing the keys and Marsha Ambrose sang her song with Nipsey's vocals in the background. She was grooving despite her watery eyes and mourning look planted on her face.

"If I die now, I made the set proud." Nipsey Hussle—*Victory Lap*

Blacc Sam, Nip's big brother, came up to share some of his memorable moments and accomplishments with Nip to the world. You never know that pain of losing a brother until it happens to you. Most of us in locked-down society knew the exact pain Blacc Sam was going thru because we can relate and personally experienced it. He said to Nip that he made the whole world proud, not just the hood. This had everyone blinking and wiping their eyes on the inside.

Blacc Sam went on to tell us how Nipsey was naturally gifted at rapping, creating music, and hustling. Also, Nipsey was really frontline pushing out there in them streets and he really rapped about the true stories he lived. It was all facts. He wanted to get Nip out the streets, so he turned him to focus more on his music. Then he wanted to build a business legit for Nip so he didn't have to worry about getting caught up. However, he didn't know Nipsey was going to end up building a business for him. Then he went on to share how Nipsey went from getting kicked out of the shopping strip where he was selling CDs out of his car to actually being able to purchase the same lot that the infamous Marathon Clothing resides on Crenshaw.

The fellas on the inside was smirking with head nods when Blacc Sam shared the story of Nip having hands after a long street brawl. Nipsey fought to the end, still on his feet. We was glad to hear all the stories but knew Nipsey walked it like he talked. I was still impressed with Nipsey's mind and dedication of putting together a hard drive and building a complete computer when he was younger by himself. Blacc Sam had to admit how shocked he was at Nip for that, too.

When they started showing all the slide shows of Nipsey's life progress and happy moments with his family and friends, it was epic pics and priceless video clips of a young Nip. It showed

Nipsey's dance moves and talent for the camera back then. He was already camera-ready. What stood out the most was when Nipsey went to the motherland to see his Eritrean family and roots. His Eritrean dad and his big brother traveled to Eritrea, Africa. It was like Crenshaw meets Eritrea because Nipsey and bro was out there with a Cali swag. Everyone could only dream of going to Africa and discovering their ancestry roots. Most of us don't leave the hood, let alone the state or country. It was uplifting to see Nip connecting with his roots.

Nipsey's dad went on to read all the Eritrean traditional burial process and help call on the ancestor gatekeepers so Nip's spirit would have a safe, easy journey into transition. His mom also helped read the names, too.

His father went on to say how strong Nipsey was and his high tolerance for pain thru all his younger surgeries and his complication when he was born. He told us why he named Nipsey Ermias and the definition and reason why he named because how strong Nip was and a survivor and fighter since day one.

Nipsey's mother surprisingly was at a peace and very calm despite the circumstances. We worried about her the most, and a mother's grief is the worst because they have mothering natural protecting spirits. She told us don't be sad and Nipsey did his Earthly duties that it was time for him to transition. His spirit needs to evolve and Nipsey's energy was everywhere and she could still feel it as she spoke. She said she was calm and at peace when the police called her and she went to the scene and didn't see no blood or they wouldn't show her the tape at the gas station.

Then she shared an amazing story about Nipsey. When he was young, her car caught on fire, and Nipsey jumped out, ran down the street in traffic to flag down a fire truck. She didn't think they would see him or stop for this little boy at the time. And Nipsey would stick his hand down there to help her take off the hot oil filter. When he came back with the fire truck, she knew Nipsey exuded true bravery. We was all smiles listening in awe.

Nipsey's close day one homegirl Nuney Loc went on to talk and shared her memories. One of the things she shared that stood out was how Nipsey would believe in her and tried to bring out the best in her, supporting her in all her endeavors. She said he would encourage her to read or go to school for it and she can work for him producing videos or whatever she decided. She said even with her cooking he would tell her she could make a killing selling because it was that good, people will buy it for real. The Bible expresses the value of a true friend. It's priceless.

When Lauren London, Nipsey's sister Samantha, his nephew, and kids came up to speak, everyone was fighting back shedding tears. It was very emotional. Lauren London had on her dark shades, holding their son, Kross. She shared how Nip would give her books to read and was her best friend that taught her and helped her on so many areas to level up and to never fold. She said she was so amazed and just loved to watch him sleep

68

so peaceful. Then how she saved his last few long text messages and reread his words of empowerment and passion. She closed saying, "The Marathon Continues" and threw up Nip's N-Hood sign. Everyone loved Lauren London representing and giving it up for N-Hood Nip.

Nipsey's nephew spoke and told his story about Nipsey called him Killa and would always say respect and taught him respect. Then he had a dream that he was swimming in the ocean and saw Nipsey and he was in heaven. He talked with so much mannerism and stood with such strong posture. Nipsey was schooling and mentoring him right. At least he will have memories of Nipsey. Lauren London said her only fear was her 2-year-old son never getting a chance to know his father.

Nipsey's sister talked and told us how much Nipsey always looked after her and took care of them. She seemed most affected. She was devastated and we could see her love and hurt. It was hard to watch because seeing Nipsey Hussle's loved ones so crushed and hurt knowing how strong his energy was with the world, especially his loved ones. My heart goes out to all of them and his loved ones that couldn't talk or attend the services. Especially his Eritrean community.

"Money, love and loyalty." Nipsey Hussle—*Victory Lap*

The rapper Y.G. and friend of Nipsey came up with D.J. Mustard to speak on Nip. He said Nipsey was his brother from another color and Nipsey was the first Crip to ever give him a book. All the Crips and Bloods were laughing and nodding their heads simultaneously. Y.G. also appeared a little tipsy, which gave it a more authentic hood love because at most hood funerals, the majority is drinking and bubbly as a pirate.

Snoop Dogg showed his love and memories. He began to tell the story how he first heard Nipsey's CD. That his homie gave Nip's CD telling him to listen to cuz he hot. Snoop said that Nipsey was from the gang but used his CD to roll some weed up on and never listened to it. Then Snoop said he told Nipsey that same story after he met him. Snoop turned around to Nipsey's casket and started talking to Nipsey, stating, "Ain't that right, Cuhz? Remember I told you that?" It was all love. He also said Nipsey would talk music and different business all the time with him before they even did tracks together.

Snoop Dogg's closing statement after throwing up N-Hood was: "God so beloved the world, he blessed us with a Crip!" I swear the concrete tiers was lit with homies rejoicing. That statement had the luvis lit and applauding. Applaud by Snoop.

The Los Angeles pastor closed, delivering a nice sermon where he segued into a metaphor about Nipsey being a whole entity like McDonald's. Most people try to duplicate to be the best rapper and have the best burger. However, Nipsey was the burger, fries, etc. When most people's focal point is one-dimensional, Nipsey was universal. Then he started paraphrasing Nipsey Hussle's *Grinding All My Life* chorus.

Nipsey had so many pallbearer homies to carry his casket out the Staples Center. Before they lifted his casket up, you saw a slew of rolling fists and 6 fingers thrown up for Nip and his affiliates. Nip had a bunch of flowers around his casket and the All Money In dollar sign emblem centered in front of his casket, too.

They took Nipsey's hearse on a route thru Crenshaw one more time for the fans and public before laying him to rest. It was jam-packed in the streets of Compton for Nip, especially the Shaw. Little kids, motorcyclists, women, and crowd was all reaching out, touching Nipsey's hearse. Everyone wanted to feel Nip's love and radiant energy and show their love and regard back. Once they hit the Marathon plaza, it was packed with people worse than L.A. traffic by the thousands. The hearse had parked, halted by the sea of endless community supporters, fans, and loved ones. It was truly an epic ending to see.

Nipsey Hussle got laid to rest at Forest Lawn, the Hollywood celebrity cemetery. May the Creator bless his spirit high. May he rest in complete harmony.

"V-12 with them racks in the middle...mmhm...hmm—Pray to God they let my dog out the kennel." Roddy Ricch ft. Nipsey Hussle

- Chapter 8 -

"Aftereffect"

"I told Khaled bounce the 4 till the bar break." Nipsey Hussle ft. John Legend—*Father of Asad*

The D.J. Khaled's latest *Father of Asad* album had a Nipsey Hussle ft. John Legend *Higher* song. This was the last video Nipsey did a few days before he passed away. It was a dope collabo and a different Nipsey Hussle sound. It had a soulful melody to it. Of course John Legend added his splash to it, creating some epic soul-touching vocals on the hook and playing the keys.

Nip had on his all-royal-blue head to toe with his hair braided back. He had the lo-lows hitting switches in the background with D.J. Khaled. Nipsey was at the top of his game and the height of his success. We been riding with Nip since his first CD and all his first videos with the long shirts and NY fitted hats and gold chains. To see his progress from then to now was truly a transformation. Nip's *Old New York* video, you can see a young hungry Nipsey that still owned his craft vs. his last D.J. Khaled ft. video. Nip looked a lot more accomplished and made, but most of all at peace. On that video you could also see how tall Nipsey actually was, too.

The video and song showed you just how versatile Nipsey Hussle was, and he could stamp any song or subject. He always had a remarkable story to tell about it. Nip broke thru contrast prisms and it showed clear as day. His passion was so evident and this is part why his legacy is so strong and unbreakable like Teflon. That's what we loved and respected about Nip, too.

D.J. Khaled donated all proceeds from Nipsey Hussle ft. song into a trust fund for Nip's kids, Emani and Kross. Khaled stated in an interview how his experience with Nipsey Hussle was. That Nip was professional and they clicked and started talking about properties and real estate, music, and their overseas background. Khaled said he could see Nipsey's foreign features and thought he was Palestinian, too. Nip told him his pops was Eritrean. Khaled went on to say how he was shocked by the news of his untimely death, but how powerful and incredible Nipsey Hussle was with music and behind the music. He said they went out to eat and Nipsey Hussle was smart and loved his city.

"I been self-made from the dribble." Nipsey Hussle—*Victory Lap*

The aftereffect of Nipsey Hussle's passing was nothing but outpours and outreaches of love, support, and dedication. You truly seen the real Nipsey Hussle effect touched by the world. From Africa to London it was so many tributes to Ermias "Nipsey

Hussle" Asghedom. Only if Nip can see how he left a mark on the world and made the whole world proud. Facts.

"No co-sign, I ain't need the radio to do mine, I did fine." Nipsey Hussle—*Victory Lap*

Nipsey Hussle was in the Top 10 radio playlist all summer long. Locked-down society was proud to hear Nip getting ample radio spins because we knew he accomplished his levels and broke thru barriers that he didn't even intend to. Plus the world could see and hear Nip's classic Crip story that so many people sell out or suppress from that environment, forgetting about the struggle and us incarcerated becoming more pop/commercial with chains shackled on them.

"That's how I knew—That's how I knew!" Nipsey Hussle—*Crenshaw*

The glass portrait of Nipsey Hussle painting, it was a bidding war between Tyler Perry and a successful black woman entrepreneur at a charity auction. She outbid Tyler Perry and was sold the Nip glass portrait for $100k. It was a masterpiece and looked like a Nipsey portrait in a mirror but transparent. Very innovative and extraordinary piece.

An NFL player did some tribute cleats for Nipsey Hussle. He designed a few different pairs and some were different color blues and airbrushed. I think that was very creative and the fact that he used his professional platform to push Nip's movement and continue the marathon despite the NFL's ongoing controversy with black street-related movements like Colin Kaepernick demonstrations.

Russell Westbrook, a good friend of Nipsey Hussle from Los Angeles and an NBA All-Star, recently went off in NBA season game. He hit a triple-double, 20 points, 20 assists, and 20 rebounds. Soon as he hit 60, he started going up shouting, "That's for Nipsey—That's for Nip!" Then he threw up N-Hood for Neighborhood Nip. You could see the emotion raging within Westbrook. It was definitely contagious. Everybody incarcerated watching knew and could feel the same emotion, but we was glad to see someone in the league brave enough to represent Nip on the court.

Other athletes like LeBron James were also seen in summer practice facilities supporting Nipsey Hussle, sporting a goldish-yellow Crenshaw hoodie with maroon letters. We were watching ESPN and seen Lebron and Anthony Davis and went berserk! It was a good look to see the King James pushing the Marathon Continues hashtag.

However, T.I., Meek Mill, and other rappers and celebrities have been showing their tributes and love supporting the Marathon Continues in Crenshaw hoodies and gear seen all over, too. It was definitely an outpouring of support reflected across the globe. It showed Nipsey Hussle's validation and that none of his arts, dedication, activism, hard work, and so much more wasn't in vain. All pure from Nip's heart.

"Add something from the art." Nipsey Hussle

The 2019 B.E.T. Awards, Nipsey Hussle was to receive the Humanitarian Award. B.E.T. also did a tribute to Nipsey Hussle, too. They did the outside red carpet all blue for Nip. It was pretty bright aqua-ish royal blue.

Inside during the awards, D.J. Khaled and John Legend performed the Nipsey Hussle feature song. They were showing clips from the last video Nipsey did with the D.J. Khaled song performing. John Legend played the piano live and sang his heart out. It was a great tribute.

Rapper and Nipsey homie Tip "T.I." Harris presented the B.E.T. Humanitarian Award for Nipsey Hussle to Nip's family and loved ones. T.I. wore a clean crispy white suit. His mannerism and speech was well delivered, and he is an immaculate crowd speaker. It didn't sound like he was reading from the teleprompter because it sounded natural and from his heart, too. He elaborated on Nipsey being a philanthropist, revolutionary, activist, humanitarian, community leader, advocate, and father.

It was a video clip of Nipsey's works, pics of him doing community engagements. A few people, activists, and business partners talked about Nipsey's goals, good deeds, business ventures, contributions, school funding in science research and computers. They talked about him leaving us a blueprint and being a radical entrepreneur. His design and art forms, connection and evolutionary progress. Intellectual properties. Timeless to his ideas, designs, and planning.

Being a visionary, prolific, inspiration, and influential. Using his words, principles, and elements as sustainability.

Nipsey did in 10 years with his vision, dedication, heart, and hard work what people couldn't accomplish in hundreds of years against all odds.

The whole place stood up on their feet, giving it up for Nipsey Hussle's loved ones and family as T.I. presented them with the award. Nipsey Hussle's kids, mom, dad, granny, sister, nephew, and Lauren London all came up and received the award, accepting it on Nipsey Hussle's behalf.

Nipsey's granny was the first to speak. She said that she was amazed of all the love and support throughout the world for Nipsey. She loves him and misses him dearly. Nipsey's mother spoke highly from her spirit and said she still didn't see the tape. Then saw Nipsey's homie outraged that day and told him it's fine, that Nipsey's spirit needed to transform and his energy is still everywhere. Nipsey's father had on the Marathon Continues hat. He said a year ago, Nipsey Hussle was performing outside. Now we all honoring him for the 2019 B.E.T. Humanitarian Award and celebrating his life. He shouted, "The Marathon Continues." Lauren London said, "The Marathon Continues," too.

Nip's sister Samantha was draped in the blue rag attire. She had that Nipsey Hussle S tatted on her face, representing. All the Crips and luv1s inside went into a frenzy again like they drunk 4 cups of Starbucks coffee.

Next Y.G. came out with two of Nipsey Hussle's N-Hood homies, performing *Last Time I Checked*. It was a half-split blue and red stage. Y.G. did his verse and the Crips and Bloods in the Penn once again was up and dancing and throwing it up for their sides and hoods, all in real respect united without conflict or bumping heads. It was big! What Nipsey Hussle's energy's everlasting effect perpetuated. Even all the reports saying all the Crip and Blood alliances throughout L.A. because of Nipsey's influence or passing is still so incredible. Of course we will not be able to cease all gang-on-gang violence, but a little progress goes a long way and stops some bloodshed to save lives. One at a time. It shows us Nipsey Hussle's reputation has huge reach and value.

"Either I'm genius or y'all helluva scary." Nipsey Hussle—*Last Time I Checked*

Long live the legacy of Ermias "Nipsey Hussle" Ashgedom... May the Marathon continue thru us all for betterment of self, communities, and us as black people as a whole.

- Chapter 9 -

"The Hoodie Nip Never Got (BDB)"

"Like Jay-Z and Nip, Hitachi got the Billion-Dollar Blueprint."
Hitachi Choparazzi—*Billion-Dollar Blueprint*

I composed that track 2 years ago. Influenced by Nipsey Hussle and Jay-Z, of course. Before Jay-Z was publicly announced a billionaire by Forbes as the first hip-hop billionaire, I already knew about his billion-dollar blueprint. I'm not referring to his *Blueprint* album. I'm talking about his actual inner blueprint.

Nipsey Hussle had his own unique blueprint, too. He definitely would have hit a billion plus, too. Him and Jay-Z had similar backgrounds, just different coasts. They both had that hustler D-boy mentality approach from their prior street experience and applied it to the rap game and the game of life. The ones aware and smart will prevail before they fail.

My cuzzo Byrd told me I didn't have to stop hustling—I just needed to switch my hustle. Meaning all that street shuffling and hustling that lands us into the Penn needs to be reevaluated and applied into a different legitimate field. He helped me thru my transformation, mentoring me to keep going straight when I wanted to backpedal.

This is what Nipsey also contributed to me and lockdown society in reforming. It's so much talent behind these walls, wasted and undiscovered potential. It's people who are prolific writers, art designers, rappers, boxers, ballplayers, screenwriters, engineers, geniuses, leaders, activists, etc. So much more that the world forgot about. It's millions of black men helluva talented locked up, not to forget about all the women facilities, too.

I believe in growth, development, and second chances to have a better chance at life, family, and liberty. I understand doing the time for your crime. However, these excessive sentences need to be abolished and reformed with a Senate bill. Most of us aren't perfect and make mistakes, learning the hard way with super-hard long time. Once we awaken and become conscious vs. subconscious in that dreamy matrix-like state, then we can spread social awareness one person, home at a time. Until we can awake as a whole and push positive energy as a whole, too.

"Black business owners doing it makeshift." Nipsey Hussle— *Victory Lap*

In history you supposed to educate yourself, read people's stories, study their masterpieces, research their methodologies, and formulate their ideologies. Learn lessons from them, observe them good or bad, including mistakes made. This why Nipsey

Hussle always enforced people to read and J. Cole said he studied the greats.

I, too, had a hustle-hustle, 'get rich by any means' street mentality until I was awakened on the inside like Malcolm X. Nipsey's music helped enlighten me, inspired me, and motivated me to think outside the box, even though I was actually inside of the box.

Nipsey influenced me with his All Money In movement back in 2015. So I started creating content and developing self-building material, then sharing with others inside. Next thing you know, I had developed and built all these businesses, brands, programs, apps, and started my own movement to push the youth.

I used my time for me, not against me, and started to reform, rethink, reassess, and rehabilitate. I couldn't not read or write shameful until I got older because I never seen the value in it past living in the streets, going to college, or living past 17 years of age. Now I have read hundreds of books, wrote over 20 books of various genres and subject lines. I started my own self-publishing Chop-a-Style company with my own literary agency. My reason is to give all people incarcerated and underprivileged with no means or funds to be published and heard. To have a voice. Everyone has a story to tell and needs help, assistance, or an opportunity to shine or elevate in their life.

What I learned most from Nipsey Hussle was discovery of individuality. I believe everyone has their own blueprint, just like everyone has their own thumbprint and unique proprietorship.

You cannot be the best Nipsey or Jay-Z. You can only be the best you and master building self to accumulate wealth. Not just monetary wealth, but wealth in spirit, wealth in health, wealth in consciousness, and wealth in executive decision making.

One of my brands I started along with a movement was the Billion-Dollar Blueprint movement, where we teach you 3 core principles of education, elevation, and innovation to help discover your own blueprint. We build on skills and development. Challenge a person to transition into their peak potential by emulating the outline principles and adopting new habits of betterment.

I believe innovators are the future, and we are all great creators and visionaries. So Billion-Dollar Blueprint movement isn't just social awareness. It is an entrepreneurship as well. It is a youth movement too that I have my sons help engage with their peers and the community, donating Billion-Dollar Blueprint shirts and hoodies to the youth, encouraging them to stay in school and discover their blueprint. I even give BDB youth modeling contracts and give them BDB certificates, too. I wanted to influence them in a positive manner, also empower them to feel their significance and that they are special and matter, just like Nipsey did directly to us, and influence the street culture with the lockdown society culture.

This all was inspired by Nipsey Hussle's movement and music. I wanted to take the time out to acknowledge Nipsey Hussle, not just because he reps the Blue Team but for his love, influence, and selfless good deeds. He passed away without the outside world knowing how much he was the face of the lockdown society reform. People didn't know or see how we had evolved and united for the best and creating businesses, chance, space and opportunity.

"I laid down the game fo y'all niggas, told y'all how to charge more than what they told y'all niggas." Nipsey Hussle—*Victory Lap*

Everyone on my social feed, homies, and loved ones knew my high regard for Nipsey. Even in my videos and raps, Nip motivated me. I took it the hardest when Nipsey Hussle passed. Mainly because of me wanting to meet and collaborate with my mentor and idol. Not on music, but on building and development of innovation. Two genius mindframes together collaborating on goal-setting and executing. Imagine Thomas Edison and Einstein on the same timeline. So when I got released finally, I wanted to give Nip a Billion-Dollar Blueprint hoodie and share my story of what him and his music helped create and me to evolve my mind habits and life. I had a checklist to who all of the influencers I wanted to send a hoodie and my back story and movement with. Also how many people I am able to influence with my movement on the inside, and outside, too, including Jay-Z on the list, but Nipsey was number one top of my list. It's hard to reach out thru emails and social site or agents if you don't have a voice or referrals. A lot of influencers wouldn't give a stranger they don't know their individual busy time or acknowledge someone incarcerated. However, I knew Nip would and was real, especially all the touching stories I seen after he passed. I was devastated when Nipsey passed because don't nobody want to see their favorite hero die in a movie or life, period. Especially if it's a relatable back story and emotion behind it.

"That's how you end up in penthouse and cars, that's how you start off a curb server and end up a star." Nipsey Hussle—*Victory Lap*

This Nipsey Hussle lockdown society book was not an easy task because how much I looked up to Nip and was really crushed by his untimely death. I know time heals all wounds, but I wanted to do our tribute to Nip and show appreciation and gratitude plus all his influential energy on the inside, too. That day needs to be highlighted that he was helping his homie reintegrate fresh out of serving 20 years. I acknowledge that.

Nelson Mandela spent 27 years locked up in African rough prison, then got out and led a large freedom campaign. He had busted up so much limestone he couldn't shed tears because his ducts tried up. That's incredible and means even if he wanted to sit around and mope, sobbing all day, his inner being was disable to not produce his emotional manifestation.

Martin Luther King, Jr. actually wrote a letter to God at the dining room table 6 years before his epic iconic "I Have a Dream" speech. He told God he was scared and wanted to quit because he was getting threats, called the N-word, and house getting cherry-bombed and vandalized.

However, he was more afraid of if he stopped...the people will stop, too. We must continue to push on our paths, goals, dreams, and missions. The believable is always achievable. Just like Nipsey showed and brought to the world thru his lenses. The power of unconscious parents and peers is contagious, and you can pick up or create lifetime habitual bad habits. We must elevate to levitate.

Nipsey studied Malcolm X tough, too. When Malcolm X was incarcerated and went thru his 180-degree transformation turnaround, he elevated, too. First he had to become conscious and then unglue himself. He worked on 3 essential principles: mind, body, and spirit. This is where he developed his name and Muslim name. Once he was released, he did the pilgrimage to the holy Mecca in the Middle East, which is a part of the Islamic pillars of faith. He became Malik Shabazz Hajji. Some Muslims don't ever make it to the Holy Mecca to participate in the Hajj. Malcolm X came back from the Holy Mecca transformed and elevated tenfold. He was pushing his energy and new movement. Remember this all started when he was incarcerated. He truly found himself and decreed his path. Nipsey Hussle and some of the greats used this blueprint. So can we incarcerated by the millions across the nation. United we stand, together we evolve.

- Chapter 10 -

"The Marathon Continues (TMC)"

"Rich gangbanger, y'all didn't know they made those." Nipsey Hussle ft. Rick Ross

The Marathon Continues Nip's legacy and aims through you individually. Own your masters so you can become your own master like Nipsey Hussle showed us. Not just your record masters or webmaster, but you must master self first. Master your skills first, taking one step and thing at a time. Then once you master the skill at hand, you can adopt and take on others.

If you want to continue of Nip's Marathon, you must understand all his narratives, objectives, and missions. Not just Nipsey's music, but what he stood for as a person and what was his cause of what he was pushing for, then the movement wave he created.

Remember, life isn't a sprint; it's a marathon. You must pace yourself first. Then know and learn yourself. The things you dislike show you who you are. Must learn your patterns and bad habits. Then see them and hold yourself accountable. After you can see and recognize your troubleshoot areas to change or correct them.

You can't have toxic people in your space to throw you off your course with their negative energy or feedback because it will weigh a ton on you and bring you down, beating you up verbally and mentally. Nothing more defiant than mental exhaustion because it causes you to freeze, stop, or have mental blockage, which is cancerous to your design path and perpetual progress.

Most people don't know how to find their passion, blueprint, niche column, or how to find it.

"It was visionary." Nipsey Hussle—*Victory Lap*

"How many niggas on ya payroll?" Nipsey Hussle

Everyone has triggers in their mind, good and bad triggers. Some emotional, some life-altering, leading to drastic changes. Even social triggers, where we get so caught up in the wave of the competitive world. Just because your parents and friends are doctors and lawyers, that don't mean you have to be and follow suit or society pressures. We all have human nature and instincts in us, but we don't have to follow. We can lead, and all are leaders of your own life and lifestyle regardless of conditions or limitation of excuses. If a blind man can still read, then imagine what you can do. If you continue to do what everyone else do, you will be like everyone else without ever seeing your sole purpose and peaking greatness.

"Dirty money get washed in royalty statement." Nipsey Hussle—*Victory Lap*

Like Nipsey discovered early on what he was supposed to do and knew what path to continuously trek on, you must do the same to continue the marathon of your life. You figure out what you're supposed to do by discovery of different things, exploring what comes natural to you than others. That driving voice inside you telling you who you are, what to do, and what is next. You must ignore negativity and self-doubt, tune out the world and listen to yourself. Follow your heartbeat because it won't deceive you nor lead you astray or in danger. Master your primary inculcates. Then you will find a primal attraction. Facts.

"Y'all niggas so surprise Tekashi told, real street niggas never fold." Nipsey Hussle ft. Rick Ross

Nip had so much passion, energy, using his voice to inspire, and leaving his mark on Earth. Making people better and never folding.

Greatness is challenging the present you to the future you to get better and make people in your life better. Nipsey's contribution and marathon is still with us and in us today.

Human nature confines us, but you can push a little further, moving past your own limits, not accepting. Greatness is you going above what you already done and stretching beyond your boundaries, betterment. Remember, gain the knowledge, apply the self-discipline, solidify your infrastructure.

I challenge you to go to college, get high school diploma, G.E.D., or an M.B.A., Ph.D. college degree. To educate yourself first in any field in your niche column.

Go outside your hood and community. Travel, learn America, or go outside the country and explore overseas. Get exposure like Nipsey Hussle did. Most people don't network or have accountability. No filters or immediate goals. You need to be informed.

Spend the quality time needed to perfecting your skilled craft and blueprint structure down with design, sound strategies, practice, and repetition. Once your infrastructure is solid first, then gain your knowledge, the know-how, plus your visuals.

Your product or vision can be great, but if your foundation and discipline isn't consistent, you cannot maintain your successful goals. The discipline to wait, to say no, to say yes.

We were truly blessed to have Ermias "Nipsey Hussle" Asghedom to learn from. Create self-value, then value to others and the community. This makes you priceless, no stipulations or price tags can be put on you or own you. This is what Nipsey implemented, naming his own price and creating self-value because his self-worth was his net worth. You can diversify, too. Value yourself and your true inner essence of self. Fruit will produce abundantly and doors will open. Always keep your spirit strong and God in your life. Prayer is power. They take God out of school, but you must keep the Creator in acknowledgement in your life and gratitude in all aspects. Without your spirit aligned with the Creator, it isn't no promised success.

"213 rest in peace, Nip, Never slip I put the C.R.I.P. in Crip." Snoop Dogg—*Count Down*

You learn more from your losses than wins. So you can profit from your losses. Don't accept what you see with your eyes—look deeper.

"Add something from the art, turn it into gold." Nipsey Hussle

The key to life is social engagement, your skills with people is number one in human nature. We are all social beings first and foremost. Supreme skilled with people, dealing with people, and networking with social engagement. Mastering your skill isn't just it, give yourself little test and shut off your internal monologue.

Building a platform with your message, you need personality. People move the needle. Nipsey applied this and stayed true to his community and the streets, then told his story that was a connection with the people everywhere going thru the struggle.

Everything has a person attached to it. It is a face or personality behind the movement, business, etc. Create your own legacy to pass it generation to generation like Nip. Stay in your lane and figure it out as you go.

Have a mission motivator like Nipsey Hussle did with the marathon and then continue the marathon and its impact. Create a culture behind mission. Focus on mission over method and process. Then stick with it.

"Courtside going viral when them punches get thrown." Nipsey Hussle

All the murals of Nipsey Hussle going up around L.A. and the world shows Nipsey Hussle's marathon continuing. Y.G. featured one in his video of Nip. It was dope. I encourage everyone to continue the marathon and Nipsey Hussle's core principles.

I had a dream the night of Nip's epic Homecoming that I wrote a movie script about his life and overcoming obstacles to all his self-taught and made accomplishments. I was skeptical because I didn't go to film school but can write scripts. Nip told me in my dream to "write ya script and represent the real, cuhz." That's how powerful his vibration and energy was after he passed, which I see and felt his mom's energy, too. And we was blessed to be able to inherit Nip's vibration while he was here.

Finally I ask everyone to support Nipsey Hussle's legacy and continue the marathon movement by learning about him as a person, community ties, youth programs, business, etc. Stream his music, listen to his interviews, and read his *Marathon* book or all the books Nipsey recommended people to read, too.

This book is my fuel to continue and push the marathon in a righteous endeavor. My contribution to Nip's legacy and speaking highly on his impact, influence, music, motivation, and being prolific in so many aspects. Not everyone can wear different hats or switch lanes open like Nip. To show the youth and lockdown society Nipsey Hussle's greatness and encourage them to seek their greatness because Nipsey showed us and the world it's all possible. So I used prison as my platform to show Nipsey's effect from the inside out because I know people from the outside hardly ever look in besides the handful doing prison reform and know incarcerated lives matter, too.

I also want to take the time out to ask people for y'all continuous prayers for Ermias "Nipsey Hussle" Ashgedom's spirit and most of all his family and loved ones still during this grieving and healing process. Send all them blessings and positive energy.

Fans turn into family in a sense to the artist and have a connection with them because they been following the artist since day 1 and loyal. Also been inspired by the artist and usually helped during transition or a rough time in their lives. I know we lost Nipsey Hussle untimely, a musical pioneer, but they lost a family member and a loved one.

I finished this book just 2 days before Nip's C-day.

"Happy 34th C-day, Nip! Rest in Paradise, Cuzzo... You made lockdown society proud, too...inspired and pushed us all...We got ya hits on repeat...Teflon luv, Luv1." Hitachi Choparazzi

This book is a tribute dedicated to Ermias "Nipsey Hussle" Asghedom's memory and legacy, AKA N-Hood Nip, AKA Nipsey

Hussle the Great, AKA Mr. Prolific. May God bless your soul and all good deeds.

#FreeHitachiChoparazzi #TheMarathonContinues

Epilogue

Nipsey Hussle was good at the power of persuasion thru his music, which was relatable to his audience of listeners, fans, and consumers mainly because Nipsey mastered his rare art form of composing realish content. Nipsey didn't just master the art of storytelling, he delivered the truth and facts without no caps (falsifying) like most rappers being superficial and being extra exaggerated about a persona and lifestyle they are not or actually lived, whereas with Nip you can just hear his language and see he was the real deal and what most rappers try to emulate or to impersonate to a tee. However, the streets, hood, and lockdown society know the difference and that Nipsey Hussle was one of ours who represented the struggle and, against all odds, rose above and made something out of nothing by himself positive, then did his great contribution to the community, loved ones, and the world. It was a true hood success story of the people's champ.

Nipsey helped us in lockdown society to start brainstorming and sharing our points of views, works of arts, and content creative and innovative. To thrive the connections and get more people to be aware and follow you. If we held on to all our unique content and never published it, we would never have impact to people and on the world.

The leaders are transformists that have visions for people to follow. Flexibility, value, problem solving, social skills, love, and friendship, support others to help them with life coaching or their endeavors. It will push them back on the righteous path of their destiny.

Data control is a big key, and technology is so far advancing, especially with A.I. (artificial intelligence) automating, which will take over 20 percent of all future jobs within next 5 to 7 years. However, our brains are not getting better because we so busy on our devices and social media that we are disengaged. We must not automate our minds and self. We touch our phones every 6 minutes, and if you have 100 Facebook friends, only 3 of them you can interface and call on during a crisis. Get off your devices and get to work. Even self-engagement leads to success. Learning and sharing what you know, then all people will start adopting the policy, recognizing and giving feedback. Same policy Nipsey instituted.

Most people seek shock value, mainly on going viral. However, the subtle art of being patient and persistent. Your value, level of detail, and attention to details along with your work ethic, matters. At some point you will discover your skill sets into one powerful thing. Your skill set will be increasing value in something else. Take what you're doing and apply it into another space. Something will catch and work out eventually if you continue to apply yourself on a marathon. Lean into who you are already instead of being like others. Remember, an art form is something you practice. Do what works for you and be the best at what you do. If everybody doing the same thing, it has no value!

Surround yourself with people and things in your interest and cup of tea or profession you want to go or be. If you want to be an engineer, go to school, read the pioneers of engineer history, and go around engineers. Same thing with social or computer analytics.

To lockdown society using their time for them versus against, continue the marathon and calculate your steps. Instead of letting jail defer your visions or methodology to possible career paths, read and reinvent yourself. Feed mind, body, and spirit.

Men of color in the broken penal system aren't given the benefit of doubt. Behind the walls and cemented steel bar cages lies the forgotten government modern-day slave of your loved ones, family, childhood friends, associates, classmates, misguided youth of communities, and the women stuck in the web of the well of the dark world of neglect. Guess what? Your life matters! I will continue to keep you all in my daily prayers and push our movement, be our voice. Spread education, awareness, and each one, teach one. United we stand, and forever will we evolve. Growth and betterment are life's main 2 pillars.

Special thanks to busy people on the outside to read this and share, help spread awareness, build, better themselves and continue Nipsey Hussle's legacy. #TheMarathonContinues

For all prison reform advocates, thanks for you guys' and girls' contribution, too. If the late Thurgood Marshall and the late Johnny Cochran were here to draft a bill, problem solve, it could be a key solution to free us all, including my miscarriage of justice in the excessive sentence error giving me more time to serve versus what the retired judge sentenced me to, which they refuse to fix and reverse to kick me out. Still I strive and wait on Supreme Court of Appeals. Blessings to all the readers.

RIP Nipsey Hussle the Great!!

"Last time that I checked, it was 5 chains on my neck...No smut on my rep...Legendary self-made progress...First you get the money and respect...Then the power and the hos come next!" Nipsey Hussle—*Victory Lap*

About Author

Hitachi Choparazzi is a New York City native, by the way of Omaha, who is currently incarcerated in level 5 solitary confinement in Florence, SMU-Eyman Complex, serving an illegal sentence awaiting on Supreme Court Appeal to correct his sentence with time served. The error forces him to serve 2 years extra.

He is an entrepreneur, tattoo artist turned author. Also the sole owner of Chop-a-Style Publishing and Productions, and the owner of Chatmon Sr. Literary Agency. He has written over 20 books and including scripts to pitch to Netflix. All this while he was incarcerated to start his reform act.

Founder and CEO of Billion-Dollar Blueprint and the BDB movement/youth movement, an innovator entrepreneurship where he believes everyone has their own blueprint, like everyone has their own unique thumbprint. Based on 3 core principles—Education, Elevation, and Innovation—which he teaches the youth and people how to format and discovery key. BillionDollarBlueprintmerch.com

The face of lockdown society movement along with the voice of lockdown society movement. IncarceratedLivesMovement. com #ILM #BDB

"I do this for y'all. I love y'all, rep y'all, and believe in y'all! I won't stop giving y'all all the raw stories as God bless them in my head. I have a hundred of them up there. Anybody that has a hot hand, send me samples or any comments, suggestions to my FB, IG Hitachi Choparazzi or email: orders@chopastylepublishingllc. com Chop-A-Style Publishing LLC and Productions. TeflonLuv!"

Hitachi Choparazzi prides himself on having his own signature Chop-a-Style where he freestyles all his books. They all rhyme with innovation and original storylines. He writes prequels, sequels, trilogies, and more. Does it for the people who love to read and for all those incarcerated in state, federal B.O.P., county, and women's facilities. FB,IG,Tiktok, Twitter, YouTube-Hitachi Choparazzi

Emails: Hitachichoparazziauthor@gmail.com
Billiondollarblueprintmerch.com

Other Books and Scripts by the Author

Non-Fiction

- How to Rap; The Elementary Teaching of Hip-Hop

- How To Tattoo & Start-Up Business

- How To Digital Detox

- How To Start-Up a Food Truck Business

- How To Stop School and Mass Shootings: Dear Parents

- Incarcerated Lives Matter: The Hitachi Choparazzi Blueprint

- How to Love

- The Switch: A Social Awareness Self-Help

- Nipsey Hussle Lockdown Society Dedication–Tribute

- If Trayvon Martin Could Talk; Injustice

Fiction

- The Eagle and Weasel (1-5 series kids' book)

- She Go! (urban novel)

- Reality Show 3D-HD (urban novel)

- Hot Thots (urban novel)

- Liqz (urban novel)

- Paranormal Whisper (horror novel)

- Pimp of Da Ratchets (urban novel)

- Pimp of Da Ratchets II Vegas (urban novel)

- Pimp of Da Ratchets 3 Orange is Da New Pimp (urban novel)

- Hitachi (urban novel)

- Penitentiary Pimp (urban novel)

- Weasel Society (urban novel)

- The Big Pep and Plucker Story-She Go! Prequel (urban novel)

Screenplays/Scripts

- Top Notch

- Hot Thots

- Pimp of Da Ratchets

- Weasel Society

- Million Dollar Games–A Secret Society

- The Eagle and Weasel (animation)

Available at Barnes and Noble and Amazon

Welcome to the exclusive lives of 4 extremely hot THOTs. This book will show you how to spot a THOT. From THOT tops to THOT flops, all the way to THOT Snaps and claps.

This book is the first-ever with a double twisted love triangle. Watch as Chicago, LA, ATL, and Seattle THOTs entwine at Coachella.

Some on fleek and some looking cheap, but they all cheat! They all commit aTHOTery with their THOTery acts, shameless.

Raunchy, with steaming hot sex scenes to sex swings. From wild threesome ménages, and twerking, to bare-it-all raw. Too hot! THOT gum pop...

This page-turner is an eye-opener to the very end, with a bombshell-dropping, shocking ending. The secret life of THOTs

Available at Barnes and Noble and Amazon

Billion Dollar Blueprint is a movement we challenge and inspire you to find your individual blueprint. Our mantra is "We believe everyone has their own blueprint like everyone has their own thumbprint". With these three core principles

Education

Elevation

Innovation

Hitachi Choparazzi is the founder and CEO. Orders available to support incarcerated businesses.

Orders available at: billiondollarblueprintmerch.com

www.ingramcontent.com/pod-product-compliance
Lightning Source LLC
Chambersburg PA
CBHW060336130626
46553CB00003B/1020